BRYANT MITCHELL

Jews and Christians

Elements of a Relationship Often Strained and Estranged

This book was professionally typeset on Reedsy.
Find out more at reedsy.com

Contents

1

INTRODUCTION

The relationship between Jews and Christians is a curious thing. Generally speaking, one party seems to rather not have the relationship at all and comports themselves accordingly, while the other party may have similar sentiments but is constrained by the essential construction of their faith to accept that the relationship exists, with or without the consent of the other party. In fact, Christians believe, despite the reticence of Jews to participate, they are destined someday to be one in Christ with at least a remnant of God's chosen people. This in itself is an irritating if not abhorrent notion for Jews to contemplate, seeing that, from their perspective, there are plenty of things not to like about Christians.

Speaking from relatively recent times, Jews may see Christians as not being terrible people, many of them having good intentions and living morally noteworthy lives. But even with present-day concerns begging to be addressed, there are also centuries of bad intentions and horrors screaming from the past that can foster a profound sense of apprehension, distrust, and disillusionment about what Christians really want from the Jewish community. Of course, Christians may respond by assuring Jews that they want nothing from them other than friendship, AND perhaps, an acknowledgment of shared roots in a rich, ancient history.

However, even this may prove problematic in that not only is there historical evidence suggesting grave hostilities originating with Christians and directed toward Jews, but the nature and content of the doctrines, creeds, and theological reasoning of the Christian faith in many ways are antithetical to that of the Jews.

This book attempts to address some of the elements that have served as a wedge between the Jew and Christian and catalyst promoting their estrangement. The collection of these elements is not intended to be exhaustive, nor the treatment of each as thoroughly comprehensive. But in this short discourse it is hoped a better understanding might be had to further the construction of a conciliatory and respectful bridge between Jews and Christians.

2

JESUS OF NAZARETH

As with most major religions, practically every fundamental aspect of the Christian faith has been debated and challenged by both non-adherents and believers alike. But no component of Christianity has been scrutinized more so than the life and times, personage, and origin of its founder, Jesus of Nazareth, known by millions of followers as the Christ. From his earliest days on earth, Jesus of Nazareth has been a controversial figure and polarizing force. Some love him. Some hate him. Some would rather not ever hear his name. Some revere his name as glorious and divine. But very few that know of Jesus, what he taught, and what he says about himself, can remain without opinion about the epicenter of the Christian movement, known as the Man from Galilee.

A Jewish Perspective

For the Jews that even acknowledge Jesus ever existed at all, he was merely a teacher who perhaps attempted to carve out a minor subset of Judaism. These efforts to gather disciples and spread a message eventually took on a life of its own, morphing into something completely foreign to the religion of the Jews, as seen by the Jews themselves. This "Christ cult", totally consumed by its originator, would be viewed as casting aside the Law of Moses, denigrating the traditions of the fathers, and finding itself dominated by Gentiles.

With that, the scenario just described may be the kinder of two narratives, as other Jews maintain Christianity to be a total fabrication having no historical or practical link to the Jewish people whatsoever. As the story goes, this Gentile religion was invented, its founder created, and New Testament texts written, all by the Romans and other Gentiles, with Emperor Constantine as chief instigator and sponsor. Consequently, as far as these Jews are concerned, Jesus was a fictional figure with no more place in reality than the main character of a Brothers Grimm folk tale-based children's story.

However, even taking some variation of the first mentioned, kindest, and certainly most prevalent of viewpoints - that Jesus did exist, but was simply a man who possibly did some community service and a few noteworthy deeds particular to a teacher's vocation - some of those who claimed him as king in the years, decades, and centuries following have done him a great disservice. Many professing Christian discipleship have not comported themselves according to the teachings of their Christ. They may not have been the most, but they were the loudest. They may not have been the masses, but they were the authority. They may not have been the most pious and zealous, but they were both influencers and devoted followers of the powers that then existed. The result of this loud, influencing authority and those, if not devoted, then fearful followers, was the representation of a Christ that the Jews wanted no part of. As one Jewish writer states,

"Growing up in a Jewish home, I was sure of two things: that Christians did not like Jews, and Jesus was not the Messiah…intermingling of the Church's anti-Jewish teaching and the resultant antisemitism it fostered is an almost insurmountable obstacle to Jewish evangelism by Christians today."

Perhaps Jews were not delivered an attractive Christ. And with a skewed rendering of just who Jesus actually is, perpetuated by the bad behavior of some of his followers, many Jews have a very soured and distasteful presumption about the one whom Christians hold dear. Whatever the reasons, it cannot be denied that such a presumption exists.

A Christian Perspective

Where Jews see a religion invented by usurping an already established faith, Christians see a continuation and logical fulfillment of that faith. Where Jews see plagiarism, Christians see as reiteration of truth, more Jewish history, and additional sacred texts written by inspiration of God. Most importantly, the one Jews may see as an imposter and counterfeit messiah, Christians see as the hope and savior of the whole world, the Lord from glory.

These stark differences between Jews and Christians are steeped in emotion, deep thought, and contradictory logic, psychology, and interpretation of scripture. But Jesus Christ as protagonist in the gospel story and great benefactor of Jew and Gentile throughout the New Testament, seen by Christians as lightning as well as lightning rod, is always the focal point, and consequently also the target. Because Christians are personally and unapologetically identified by their relationship with Jesus Christ, any disdain or displeasure one might have with them can easily find itself directed at him. And yet the life of Christ, by any verifiable account, is one consumed with the welfare of mankind at its most essential levels. Devotion to a holy, just, and righteous God, sacrificial love for one's neighbor, peace on earth and goodwill toward men – these are the ideals Jesus taught and brought to the world, meant to be disseminated by believers and perpetuated to the end of days. How could anyone have issues with such a person?

A major problem again may come down to the followers of Christ, and not the person of Christ. In the words of Mahatma Gandhi as recorded by Christian missionary James E. McEldowney:

"I know of no one who has done more for humanity than Jesus. In fact, there is nothing wrong with Christianity, but the trouble is with you Christians. You do not begin to live up to your own teachings."

Let us consider however, that in even a limited and summary review of passages found in the Torah, Prophets, and Writings, we find God's chosen people displeasing Him a great deal of the time. And yet, the failures of the Hebrew nation to fulfill and live out the teachings delivered to them in no way diminishes the majesty, magnificence, and absolute holiness of the Almighty. The same principle can be true of any teacher/student, master/disciple relationship. It is certainly true of that of Christ and Christians.

3

HISTORICAL TENSIONS

From common human respect, tolerance, and tentative sociability, to mistrust, antagonism, and gross inhumanity, the scope of Jewish/Christian relations throughout their collective history has been large and wide. In the German Catholic Oskar Schindler, we see the great humanitarian story of over 1100 Jews saved from the Nazis during the Holocaust, dramatically depicted in the Steven Spielberg directed film Schindler's List. And yet, countless other Jews have been harmed by some professing Christ as savior.

At the same time, long-stoked hostilities from Christianity's earliest days of being persecuted, along with the notion that it was the Jews that crucified their savior, results in a persistent animosity among many. Some might suggest the magnitude of the suffering of Christians as opposed to that of Jews may be far from equal, at least as far as numbers are concerned. Even so, there should not be any dishonor done to victims by employing the pettiness of even attempting to calculate which individuals have suffered more injustice. The moral outrage of one innocent person being violated should not be diminished whatsoever, though a 1000 of another group be found in a similar state. Suffice it to say, there is a long history of issues that have contributed to strained relations between Jews and Christians, both sides having contributed to that strain to one degree or another.

Attributed to the Jews

The Crucifixion of Christ

Perhaps the worst and most wide-spread epithet of defamation hurled toward a Jew from a Christian is the term "Christ-killer". The fact that this term was ever used by a large number of people over a significant period of time unfortunately is not surprising, given that human nature finds it much easier to perpetuate an ugly accusation as truth rather than research a matter in order to make realistic conclusions. If Christians basically have the New Testament scriptures as their source, it is easy to see how nowhere near all or even most of the Hebrew nation was instrumental in the violent, horrible assassination of Jesus Christ. Why then should anyone with just a drop of Abraham's blood be subject to such slander?

Nevertheless, the notion that Jews instigated the torture and murder of their leader, regardless of the fact that crucifixion was a purely Roman invention and solely executed by them, has sadly been for some Christians a rallying cry and illegitimate justification for hatred and prejudice. It is however encouraging that the vast majority of Christians reject these sentiments, including the Catholic Church in, amongst other places, statements found in the Second Vatican Council. Instead, the crucifixion is seen as not simply necessary for the salvation of the world, but the failure of a few Jewish men in leadership along with those that acquiesced to that leadership, which can and has happened within every group of people imaginable.

Persecution of the Church

Unlike the Crucifixion, there are many and varied sources describing the persecution of Christians. However, this persecution was perpetrated by far by Gentiles, not Jews. Namely, demented and barbaric emperors of Rome who exercised severe persecution against all claiming allegiance to Christ. Nevertheless, Jews were not without contribution to the total maltreatment and disenfranchisement of the early church, even against their fellow Jews who were followers of Christ. Accounts of these persecutions have been a rigorous part of Christianity's official history. Unintended and certainly unwelcome as it was, it's even described as being instrumental in the proliferation of the gospel. This early persecution of the church as recorded in Christian sacred texts has only added to the inherent animosity of some toward the Jewish people.

Attributed to the Christians

The Crusades

To many, the Crusades are synonymous with Roman Catholic imperialism. Directed mainly at Muslim strongholds in the Holy Land, Jews nevertheless were not exempt from the atrocities perpetrated by the crusaders. Militarizing the church in Europe during medieval times caused significant distress to Jewish communities in the form of massacres, looting, and forced conversions to Christianity. It might even be said that the Crusades served as catalyst for further desensitization to the already existing antisemitism.

The Inquisition

The infamy of the Crusades, at least as far as violently forced pledged allegiance to the church is concerned, was perhaps surpassed by the notorious Inquisition. Jews were hardly the only group suffering the horrors of the Inquisition, but they certainly experienced their share of abhorrent cruelty at the hands of Catholic persecutors.

The Holocaust

Despite courageous efforts by some to help them in their desperate plight, the Holocaust is without question one of the worst examples of persecution directed specifically toward Jews ever experienced in their history. But along with the debased operations of Hitler's "Final Solution" is the shameful behavior of the Roman Catholic Church in their quiet pacifying, if not corroborate, dealings with Nazi authorities. This period of the church's history was addressed by Pope John Paul II as he offered a formal apology on behalf of the Catholic Church for a lack of protest and humane actions not taken. Even so, the apology was viewed as inadequate by Jewish leaders, seeing that the failings of the one heading the church at the time, Pope Pius XII, were not addressed, along with the antisemitic viewpoints taught and behaviors actively performed during the war.

4

MY FAITH, YOUR FANTASY

While the Exodus for Jews and the Crucifixion/Resurrection for Christians, with all the dynamics and subplots surrounding those events, may prove seminal to the respective faiths, the Exodus is received with reverence by Christians, while the Resurrection, and even the crucifixion by some, is vehemently denied by Jews. Nevertheless, because the Jews were entrusted with the oracles of God, and the workings of the Almighty were seen through a people he chose, Gentiles drawn to the God of Abraham, Isaac, and Jacob have also, at least in recent times, sought amicable relations and even kinship with the offspring of these venerable patriarchs. However, there are reasons why those sentiments are not shared, and the notion of kinship is rejected.

Abraham and Moses

Abraham represents the natural blood lineage, a traceable genealogy that connects a person as progeny of the Father of Faith. Abraham had proven his faith by his willingness to offer up his only son Isaac. God in turn reiterated his promise to Abraham to multiply his descendants like the stars in the sky and the sand on the seashore "...because you have done this and have not withheld your son, your only son...." These natural descendants have persisted throughout the centuries, as even today, one path to Israeli citizenship is by ethnic descent - showing a bloodline to Abraham.

Moses represents the Sinai Law and the first five books of the written Torah, or in its most restricted sense, simply The Torah. He of course has an esteemed presence in Judaism, being the Almighty's chosen conduit for the people to receive both oral law and written scriptures. Consequently, there is arguably no other prophet to rival Moses in importance as far as laying the foundational basis for Jewish culture, religiosity, sacred ceremonial conduct, and godly reverential perspective is concerned.

As many Jews may see it, Christians have no part in either Abraham or Moses, for though one may not actively practice the faith, he can be connected by blood. Or, though one may not be connected by blood, they can follow the path of Ruth as a proselyte fully embracing the Jewish faith and find connection. But a Gentile Christian having not the blood of Abraham or the Law of Moses is in no way connected. Instead, they are a usurper perpetrating a fraud by claiming connection to Abraham and theological respect for Moses.

Since there is no common bloodline for which to base kinship with Abraham, such a claim undoubtedly fails. And their honored respect for Moses rings hollow seeing that the dictates instituted through Moses go largely ignored. Christians' own scriptures claim that Jesus said, "If you love me, keep my commandments." Moses might so likewise admonish them, "If you respect me and Him that gave me the law, then keep that law." As doing so would contradict major tenets of their faith, there seems to be no place for Moses in doctrinal adherence or fundamental theology. Also, it is pure fantasy for Christians to claim a relationship with and even sing of "Father Abraham" and him having many sons, for they certainly are not among those many sons.

Not A Natural Branch, But Grafted In

As Christians see it, though they are not natural branches, by nativity nourished through the root of the olive tree - good, green, and planted by the Lord God himself - they are nevertheless partakers of the spiritual life coming from that same root and divine source that established the root. For those having faith in the person and work of Jesus Christ have an efficacy that transcends the indigenous benefits restricted to Abraham's natural lineage. Now the wild branches have been cut off from their previous stock and grafted into the good olive tree and its blessed line of spiritual nutrition.

This grafting in no way nullifies, transfers, or inhibits the covenant promises made by God through Abraham to his descendants. Despite a misinterpretation and/or deliberate misguidance and misrepresentation of God's intentions by some Christians, the Jews are still God's chosen people and will remain so until the end of days. Any promise made by God will be a promise kept, as no power exists anywhere in the cosmos that can stay the hand of the Almighty.

And yet, this grafting of Gentiles affords them a sharing and common kinship with Abraham. Although there are particulars of God's covenant with Abraham reserved especially for the fruit of his loins, those with faith in Christ travel through Abraham, pass the curse levied against the parents of all mankind and consequently, their children, to the promise of deliverance and a right to the Tree of Life.

Moses also, having a role specific to God's chosen, produced a law not to be abolished, but fulfilled in Christ. Christians see the spiritual essence of the Law vividly coming alive in the teachings of Jesus. God was always meant to be loved by his creation with all their heart, mind, and soul. And a brother was never meant to have hatred in his heart for his brother, but to love him with the same fervency as he does himself. In slaying his brother, Cain set precedence not in receiving consent and affirmation, but derision and condemnation. So, the command to "love thy neighbor" covers the entire scope of the righteous designs of man's interpersonal relationships with his kind. Therefore, in the lives they live and the godly intentions of their hearts, Christians honor Moses and revere the One who established the holy tenets through Moses.

5

RESILIENT PROSPERITY

Resilient Jews

One component of Jewish dynamism is their resilience in not simply surviving as a people, which alone is remarkable, but also how they have thrived throughout the years in work and industry. Jews have found themselves highly proficient and thereby prosperous in professional careers, technical skills, and vocational trades, despite persecution, displacement, dispersion, and even attempts at genocide. How have they done it, seeing that many other ethnic groups have been totally lost over the centuries, or at least lost their homogeneous identity by being overtaken and assimilated into larger more dominant groups?

There are a few theories, but one rather radical but very plausible idea is versed by economists Maristella Botticini and Zvi Eckstein in their book, *The Chosen Few: A New Explanation of Jewish Success*. They suggest the Roman destruction of the Jerusalem Temple in 70 CE caused not only a massive dispersion of the Jewish population, but a dismantling of the religious, social, and authoritative order existing in the form of high priests and other religious elites. The authority previously found in Jerusalem has now shifted to local rabbis, with the novel requirement

15

and expectation of "…every Jewish man to read and to study the Torah in Hebrew himself and, even more radically, to send his sons from the age of six or seven to primary school or synagogue to learn to do the same." This new standard of literacy in a vastly illiterate world would prove transformational for Jewish prosperity in the centuries to follow.

Whatever theory or combination of theories may be true, the historical fact remains that through massacres, plagues, rise and fall of empires, etc., Jews have consistently found significant accomplishment and success.

But though their perpetual prosperity is welcomed and celebrated amongst themselves, it has many times caused envious eyes and jealous hearts from outsiders. The result has been foul intentions to unethically, deceitfully, and even forcefully misappropriate and confiscate their wealth. The more prosperous they become, the more conspiratorial others are toward that prosperity, all in efforts to reduce their economic strength and stem the perceived threat of a "takeover".

Christians of Privilege

"Jews will not replace us!"

There is a not-so-subtle hint of merited privilege in the dogmatic proclamation, "Jews will not replace us!" It also conjures questions of who the "us" is and what the "replacement" means. The identity of the "us" perhaps can be determined by examining the persons making the proclamation, while what the replacement entails can be deductively revealed to mean one group assuming the social, political, and authoritative status of another. Of course, along with this sense of privilege comes an anxiety and fear of loss directed toward any perceived threat - negative emotions that drive many hateful and violent behaviors.

This and other antisemitic rallying cries made in the fervor of American White Nationalism, an ideology whose ire is directed toward a number of other groups besides Jews, namely Black Americans, is easily lumped together with the ultraconservative rhetoric of White Christian Nationalism. Participants in the deadly 2017 "Unite the Right" protests in Charlottesville, Virginia displayed swastikas while chanting a host of debased slogans drenched in Nazism. But mingled with other ethnic slurs, are they so far removed from the language and ideology espousing a threat to pure Americanism said to be caused by those "other-than" – other than white, other than Christian?

Christian Nationalism claims primarily that 1) the United States was founded as a Christian nation, and 2) the notion of a separation of church and state is not based in constitutional precepts and is far from the intent of the founding fathers. That is, as Samuel L. Perry and Andrew L. Whitehead describe it, "*… an ideology that idealizes and advocates a fusion of Christianity* with American civic belonging and participation….*" (The asterisk denoting something other than orthodox Christianity.) In other words, the United States is now a Christian nation, always has been, and its citizens should make every effort to make sure it always will be. Not only that, but accepting the fact that the nation has within its borders the "other-than", they see it as necessary and wholly proper that these certain groups recognize and conduct themselves according to their "place" in the social order. Also, Christian Nationalist proponents seem to portray an almost pubescent naivete by believing lives, behaviors, and possibly even thoughts will change by molding the political landscape into their image. With this understanding of the thought processes of many citizens, even some occupying the highest levels of American government, it's not difficult to see how Jews and other groups, whether real or imagined, can FEEL marginalized and see themselves viewed as not being fully integrated as American. And this radicalized and perverted sense of nationalism isn't reserved for America or the 21st century. It has previously been seen in other nations and empires of the world and times of the past. But the contemporary occurrences in America offer a vivid visual aid to the tensions between Jews and Christians and the complexities thereof.

American Christian Nationalism is merely the conflict-inducing "flavor of the month" used to seize political power for the purpose of advancing its own ideals; to exclude the undesirables and identify the "good citizens", the rightful heirs to constitutional rights and privileges; and to prioritize the viewpoints of "genuine" patriots, in this case, the "real Americans". The criteria used by Christian Nationalists in this vetting process does not appear to be based on law-abiding, civic-responsible citizenship, but rather ethnicity, political positions, cultural perspectives, and religious affiliation. However, there is a stark difference between Christian Nationalism with its relationship to, and even underpinnings of White Supremacy, and the true, authentic faith of Christianity.

Mainstream pastor and theologian John MacArthur said, "There is no such thing as Christian nationalism." "So the idea that you should link up some political effort, some political process, some social process, some gain of power or influence in a culture as part of the advance of Christianity is alien to Christianity."

He is not alone in his denouncement of Christian Nationalism.

"Christian nationalism wraps the Cross in a flag and thereby suggests America has replaced biblical Israel as God's chosen people. This is poor theology and comes dangerously close to idolatry." - Ronald S. Cava

"They have fused Christianity with our national culture in ways that tarnish the essence of authentic faith in Jesus." - John Whitsett

Among those professing Christian affiliation and not necessarily Chistian discipleship, there is, and has been for centuries, an air of Christian privilege that seeks to exert its own self-interested interpretation of divine commands as well as gain secular and materialistic prosperity at the expense of other groups. All the while they ignore the antithetical trappings this mentality has to Christ and his teachings. One can only hope that this distorted religious and sociological view can be reduced to a small pus-filled pimple on the backside of Christendom waiting to be lanced and cleansed. Nevertheless, as long as it does exist, it will contribute to strained relations between Jews and Christians.

6

ALOOF JEWS/OBNOXIOUS CHRISTIANS

No Proselytizing

There are various reasons why Jews, for the most part, do not proselytize, that is, actively seek out and encourage non-Jews to convert to Judaism. Notwithstanding historic imperialism and conquest, the Christians, Muslims and other groups altruistically compelling others to join their respective faiths do so with the intention of opening a door to paradise that is presently closed to those who do not believe as they do. Jews don't necessarily see things that way. Believing instead, simplistically speaking, that any non-Jew that is a good person will also have a piece of paradise. The compulsion therefore to seek out and "save the world" does not carry the same weight and meaning with Jews as it would with others. Also, with the intense persecution Jews have experienced in the past, it's understandable why they may decide, in essence, to keep to themselves, "you don't bother me, I won't bother you."

Unfortunately, Jews may therefore appear aloof and unconcerned about the welfare of anyone but themselves. But experience shows that they are very warm-hearted and jovial people, even commanded to be kind and not mistreat strangers. As the ways and traditions of different cultures and ethnicities can always be misunderstood, the "live and let live" attitude of many Jews can often be misinterpreted to mean haughty, standoffish, and unapproachable. And yet, there is a responsibility on both sides of an engagement to offer an open-palmed salute, showing no weapons or hostile intent, only aspirations of friendship and neighborly acquaintance. Those of reasonable disposition would surely respond in kind.

Aggressive Evangelizing

On the other hand, Christians see a moral responsibility, a divine mandate even, to evangelize and spread the good news that a savior has come into the world. A nightmare for Christians is to see someone in a horror movie of a dream look up from the torment and condemnation of a wretched afterlife and say, "You said you loved me, but you didn't tell me about Jesus." The frightful dread of such a notion is what compels many Christians to evangelize, even to Jews. But, considering all well intentions, it's not difficult to see how demeaning and offensive this can appear to Jews, especially when they may see Judaism as the religion that birthed these "upstarts" to begin with. It's like the disciple trying to show his teacher the path to enlightenment.

But despite this, Christians today professing concern for Israel and love for her people, and the aforementioned nightmare throwing fuel on the fire, continue to evangelize where Christian evangelism is not welcome. This "love" is met with mild irritation by some Jews, and harsh retaliation by others. To some degree, both sides may understand the position and motivations of the other, but it seems for the most part to be a classic case of an irresistible force meeting an immovable object. Time will only tell the results of these encounters, but the evangelism of disciples of Jesus just shows one more aspect of the long-existing conflict experienced between Jews and Christians.

22

7

CONCLUSION

The issues and concerns so far listed are only some of the elements of a Jewish/Christian relationship that over the years has been strained and sometimes estranged. Curiously, one with no affiliation to either group could very well look on with bewilderment at one party desiring and claiming to be part of another party's family, if only cousins from a separate and distinct household. At the same time, members of the family so fervently desired, deny kinship, but are willing to accept others as having their own family. In other words, "you be you, and let us be us." The cloudy focus of the befuddled onlooker may eventually clear up as he comes to what he feels is a reasonable and prudent conclusion – "Why not just show one another respect, express well-wishes for each other, and move on to live separate and prosperous lives?"

But as reasonable as this may sound, a shared history and future trajectory, at least from one perspective, insists on relationship in one form or another. Christians cannot and will not, just let Jews be. If necessary, they may love, assist, and bless from afar off, but love, assist, and bless Israel they must. For one day, all God's children shall come together and worship him who is glorious and true. From their point of view, this position is carved in stone and cannot be altered. Certainly, past experiences weigh heavily on the possibility of future camaraderie, and many of the glaring differences heretofore mentioned remain. But the healing poultice of time coupled with consistent goodwill makes that future fellowship more and more a distinct possibility.

8

RESOURCES

Ministries, S. a. C. P. (2024, March 18). Jewish Evangelism in light of a negative history - Chosen people ministries. *Chosen People.* https://chosenpeople.com/jewish-evangelism-negative-history/

E. McEldowney, J. (1997, August). *My visit with Mahatma Gandhi.* Internet Archive Wayback Machine. Retrieved November 11, 2024, from https://web.archive.org/web/20210328011736/http:/people.virginia.edu/~pm9k/jem/words/gandhi.html#expand

Lancaster, L. (2024, October 25). *7 Specific church traditions.* Catholic Answers. https://www.catholic.com/magazine/online-edition/7-specific-church-traditions

Drozdiak, W. (1998, March 16). VATICAN APOLOGIZES TO JEWS: CHURCH CITES FAILINGS IN FIGHTING HOLOCAUST. *The Washington Post.* https://www.washingtonpost.com/archive/politics/1998/03/17/vatican-apologizes-to-jews/ce5ea6e9-bd97-4022-b639-288342b63455/

The Chosen Few: A new explanation of Jewish success. (2013, April 18). PBS News.

The long, ugly antisemitic history of "Jews will not replace us." (n.d.). November | 2021 | the Jewish Experience | Brandeis University. https://www.brandeis.edu/jewish-experience/jewish-america/2021/november/replacement-antisemitism-sarna.htmlhttps://www.pbs.org/newshour/economy/the-chosen-few-a-new-explanati

Djupe, P. A. (2020, February 5). *Christian nationalism talks religion, but walks fascism.* Religion in Public. https://religioninpublic.blog/2020/02/05/christian-nationalism-talks-religion-but-walks-fascism/

Brown, J. (2024, March 13). John MacArthur denounces Christian nationalism as "faulty viewpoint" linked to postmillennialism. *The Christian Post.* https://www.christianpost.com/news/john-macarthur-denounces-christian-nationalism-as-faulty.html

Cava, R. S. (2024, July 8). *Christian nationalism: A Baptist evaluation and response – Baptist News Global.* Baptist News Global. https://baptistnews.com/article/christian-nationalism-a-baptist-evaluation-and-reponse/?gad_source=1&gclid=Cj0KCQjwvpy5BhDTARIsAHSilynOpcxQ2kLH54sQIVyqvGgIqz4x4maISRlyDLbobaTCuQ3sY4R0YrIaAlM4EALw_wcB

Whitsett, J. (2023, July 3). *Authentic Christianity vs. Christian Nationalism — Kingdom Thoughts and Reflections.* Kingdom Thoughts and Reflections. https://www.johnwhitsett.com/blog/authentic-christianity-versus-christian-nationalism